ANIMAL THEME ADULT COLORING BOOK

Gail Kamer

All rights reserved.

Above and front cover credit: Bigstockphoto.com: Bimbimkha- 105327353

Illustration credit: Bigstockphoto.com: Panki- 128504084

Illustration credit: Bigstockphoto.com: Sybirka-121616690

Illustration credit: Bigstockphoto.com:Sybirko- 120093035

Illustration credit: Bigstockphoto.com: Viacheslav Dubrovin- 132020405

Illustration credit: Bigstockphoto.com: Peliken- 140855951

Illustration credit: Bigstockphoto.com: Sybirko- 120072879

Illustration credit: Bigstockphoto.com: AnVino- 136515515

Illustration credit: Bigstockphoto.com: panki- 128504012

Illustration credit: Bigstockphoto.com: panki- 116685575

Illustration credit: Bigstockphoto.com: Alexsnail: 122162562

Illustration credit: Bigstockphoto.com: Son 80: 124247138

Illustration credit: Bigstockphoto.com: Son 80: 124247276

Illustration credit: Bigstockphoto.com: AnVino: 140298431

Illustration credit: Bigstockphoto.com:

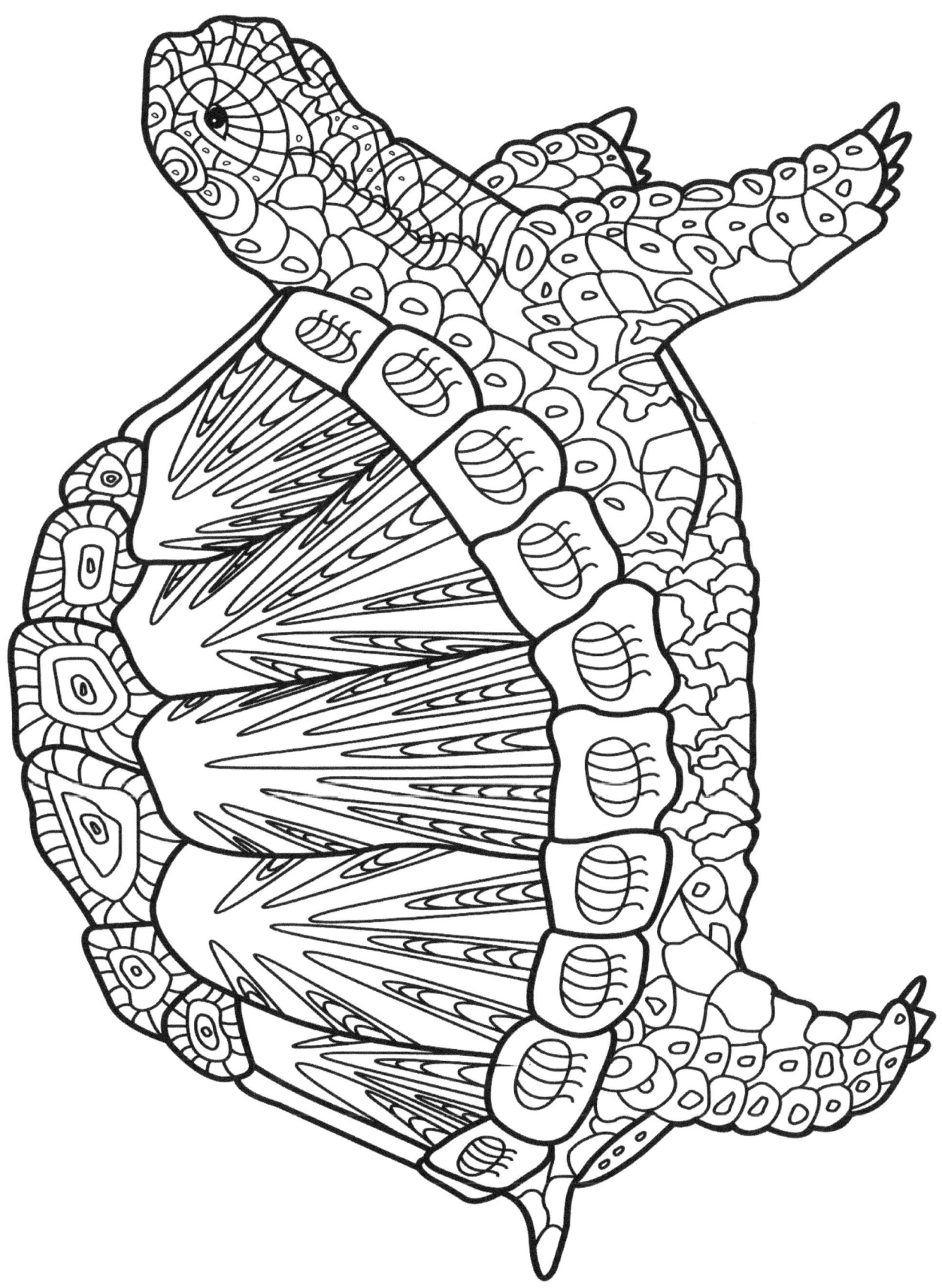

Illustration credit: Bigstockphoto.com: Sybirko: 121616612

Illustration credit: Bigstockphoto.com: Alexsnail: 119578928

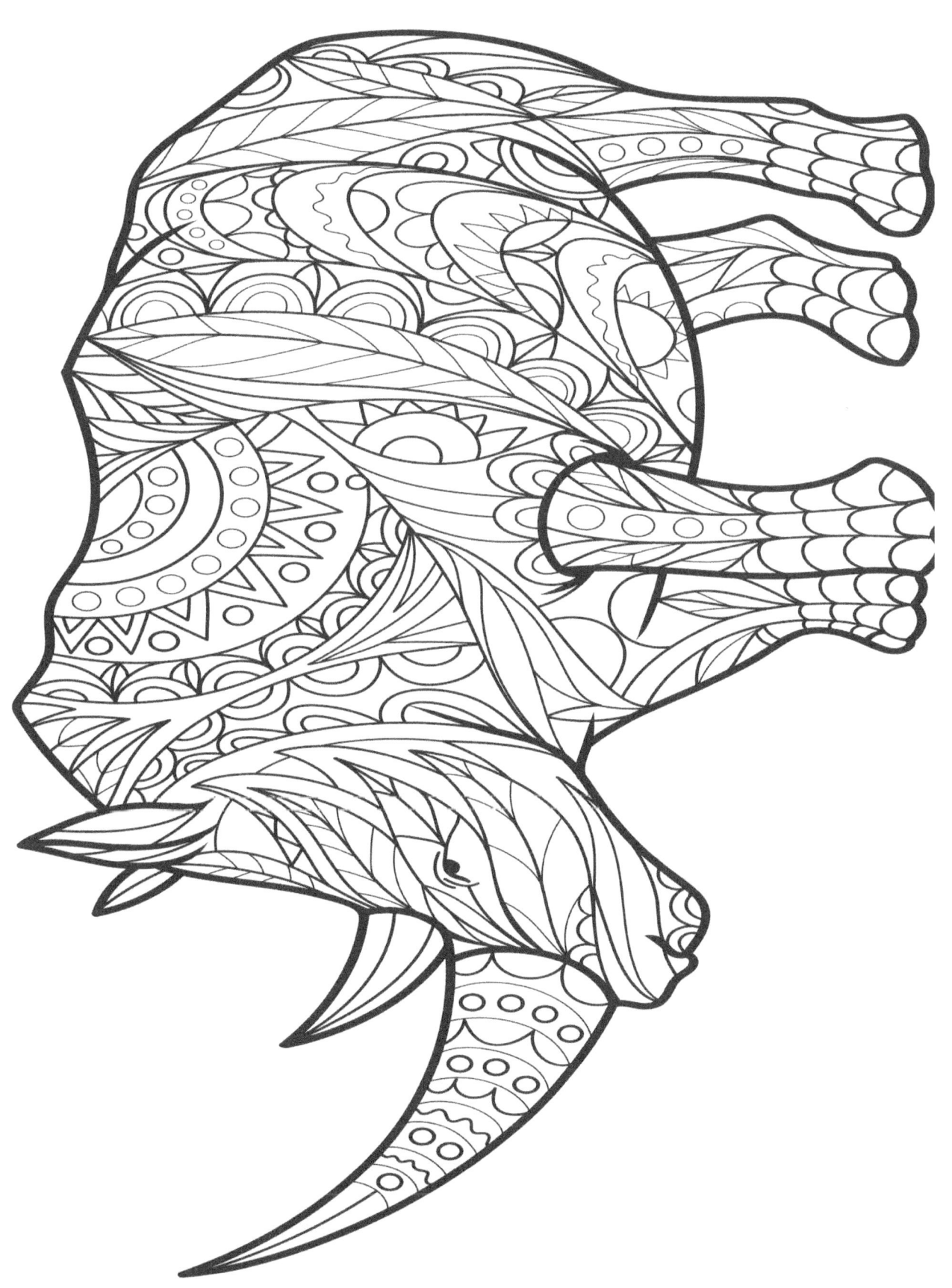

Illustration credit: Bigstockphoto.com: Alyonka_lis- 114105431

Illustration credit: Bigstockphoto.com: toricheks1 135780095

Illustration credit: Bigstockphoto.com: Dina_Asiliva- 115740554

Illustration credit: Bigstockphoto.com: Sybirko- 121616555

Illustration credit: Bigstockphoto.com: Viacheslav Dubrovin- 132020393

Illustration credit: Bigstockphoto.com: Viacheslav Dubrovin- 132020366

Illustration credit: Bigstockphoto.com: panki- 116673524

Illustration credit: Bigstockphoto.com: totally pic- 1286302222

Illustration credit: Bigstockphoto.com: Bimbimkha_ 107823223

Illustration credit: Bigstockphoto.com:Sybirko- 137593682

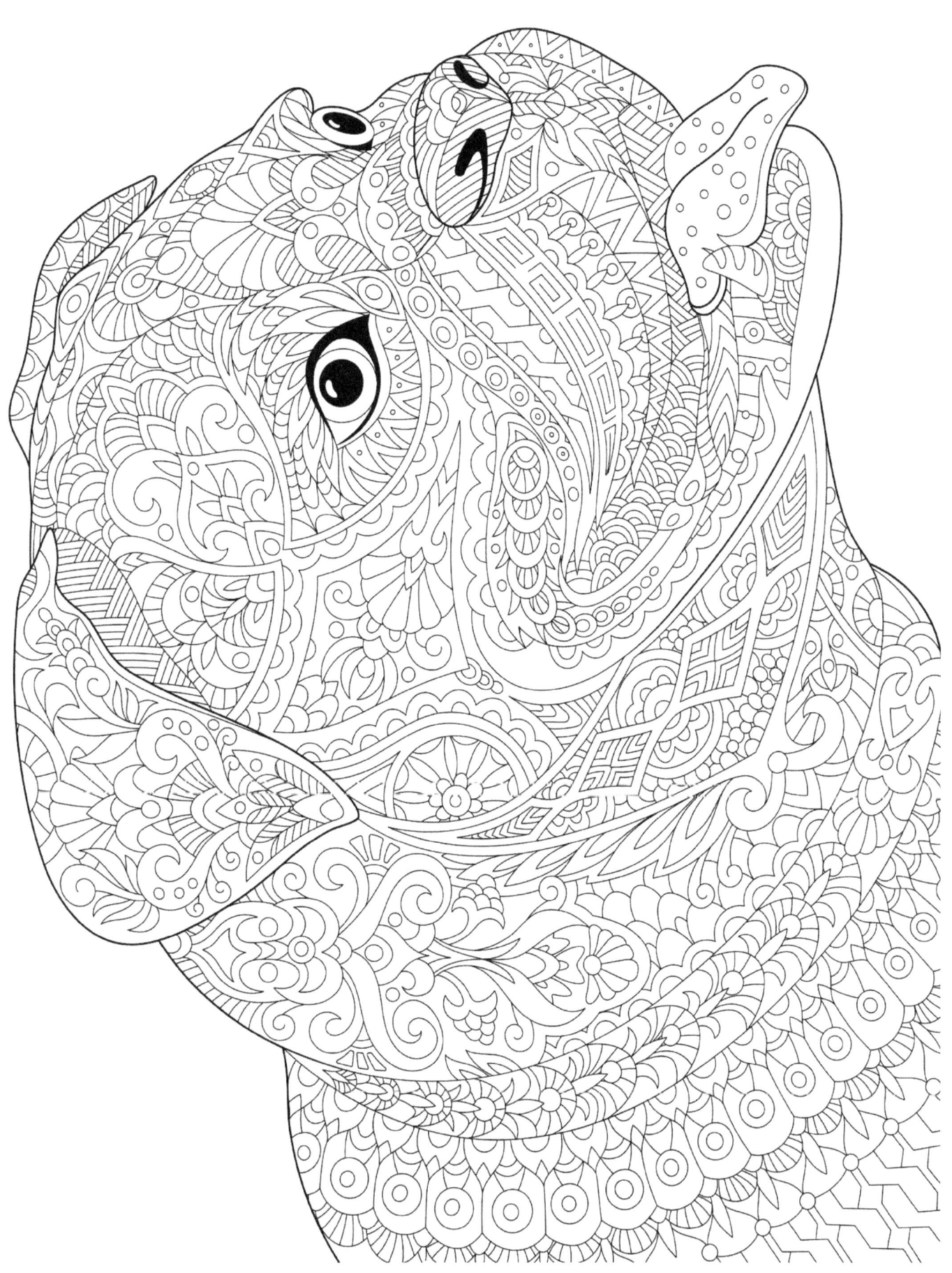

Illustration credit: Bigstockphoto.com: Bimbimkha- 113906165

Illustration credit: Bigstockphoto.com: torickeho- 131012282

Illustration credit: Bigstockphoto.com: Sybirko- 121615805

Illustration credit: Bigstockphoto.com: Sybirko- 123939137

Illustration credit: Bigstockphoto.com: Bimbimkha- 105327353

www.ingramcontent.com/pod-product-compliance
Lightning Source LLC
Chambersburg PA
CBHW080544190526
45169CB00007B/2622